GW00771946

in case of emergency press

We are proud to acknowledge the Traditional Owners of country throughout Australia and to recognise their continuing connection to land, waters, and culture. We pay our respects to their Elders.

We support recognition, reconciliation, and reparation.

Red Rite Hand

Adrian Harte

in case of emergency press
https://icoe.com.au
Travancore, Victoria
Australia

Published by in case of emergency press 2023

ISBN: 978-0-6456382-9-5

Cover design: Ward Nikriph

Acknowledgements

Sixty-seven storks, Found, Murder of Crows in Roi Fainéant Press, April 2022.
The homing, published in Abridged no. 87, May 2022.
Ibex Cry, published Beyond Words, Issue 27, June 2022
On weather, published in Embryo Concepts Zine, Issue #5, June 2022.
Line in the Sahara Sand, published in Peregrine Journal, autumn, 2022.
Red rite hand, published by Vita Poetica Journal autumn 2022
Die or Pause published by Ded Poetry, October 2022.
Things Falling Apart, Death by Black Tar, Elegy for an Empire published as part of *The Last Sermon* in Abridged, no 92, December 2022.
Silent Echoes of Prangins, published in Abridged, no.92, December 2022.
Viscious, published in Beaver magazine, winter 2023.
Shards Much Sharper than the Others, published in Fig:Ment January 2023.
Objets Perdus, Unspecified Environmental Disaster II, Lives are Little Things published in A New Ulster, January 2023.
Heart of a Girl I, Electric Dreams, The Idiot's Guide to Suicide, Never Let Go, The Stone in My Shoe published by The Awakenings Review, Vol 10, No 1, March 2023.
I Will be the Stone, published by Rabble Review, Vol 8, April 2023.
The Trials of Tutankhamun published in Tutankhamun: Wonderful Things (Black Bough Poetry) 2023.

to Christel, Eloïse, and Elliott,
and all the Harte family.

Table of Contents

Red Rite Hand

Adrian Harte

i

sermon in the suicide

Red Rite Hand

Heads down all around.
Pressed trousers
creased by the hassock
until the Great Amen.
Suffer little children,
but when praying
only so much. I never liked
call and response
from Father Flood to Moby Grape.

> And also with you.
> Lord have mercy.
> Twice have mercy.

I knew these lyrics by rote,
a shit-scared of God scrote.
His words were made flesh
and were more real than Dylan
or Didion or Dio.
May the Lord accept
the sacrifice at your hands.

My father's razor
every Saturday, my weekly bath.
Obedient son, I'd press
the blades
on my right
upper arm.

Blood will be poured
out for me and for
many, for the forgiveness
of sins. Eleven-year-old me
is wholly sacrifice. Gullible
gambolling lamb of God.

Heart Of A Girl I

This is from my Achilles op:
I trace the seam of my lower left leg
Yes, *that is my appendix scar:*
a faded path on a forest
floor. *And these ones, Daddy?*
She points to an Ogham-etched arm.
I don't answer.
A stammer too far.

She sees the world in shades
of wet-on-wet colours,
vermilion and violet.
I'm Degas-drawn
line after line after line
for penance and pain
that catch an instant.
Raw canvas shows
through hatched pink pastel.
Then, she crashes in
to my disarmed chest

her hot heart
tincturing.

Objets Perdus

A scuffed to its silver
skin red water bottle.

A size thirty-three white
and grassed green Nike shoe.

An Elsa and faded Anna
violet lunchbox, apple stalk still inside.

Objets oubliés. But that's not you.
Objets perdus. Yes, me and you.

Behind sliding glass
there is one cricket pitch,

two basketball courts,
no you shining

the hard maple floor.
Flinging yourself into the air.

Hitting balls into nets and baskets.
Crashing off and into wood.

Lost: white and red and
never roams.

Lost: we miss her very much
and need to see her home.

Lost: unfamiliar with humans.
Cash reward.

A Light Year Heavier

When the ups stop
she stalks me all the drain me
afternoon. Oh, to have the body
that sucks coffee and cigarettes.
And nothing.

Not pills, spit, and sweat.
I'm a light year heavier. Everyday.
The sign in the hospital common
room where no one goes to play piece-less
jigsaws says:

You have the right to know where you are
and, *You can be detained*
if you have a mental disorder
and, *Breakfast is*
no longer served here from six am

I no longer have tubes of Pringles,
dead English books, or teeth-cracking ginger
nuts. No visitors allowed, my world
is a ward. I obsess about getting
a room to myself. If I'll be bussed
or taxied to ECT.

If anyone will notice I'm gone
a while before I make it to the train tracks
where deer mooch in wild garlic
behind the chain link fence.

In a rusting vending machine
I find four fingers
wash them down with Listerine.
Who needs caffeine
or cigarettes when your entrails boil
and your god's long gone?
Memory is shocked astray
the lightest breeze
seizes all light
blows shrunken flames away.

Shrink

His fingers push back black keys
I look at the back of black,
screen and head blank.
                    And thumbs. Long thumbs.
Longer than any finger,
they are ballast and balance.
I talk at the screen, the head,
the lean fingers nod, tap
                    the mean thumbs do not.

A tight leather chair mumbles:
hospital, shakes, shapes,
stutters: ups, what if it doesn't stop?
The fingers tap.
                    One elongated thumb stands
guard, while the other twiddles.
Oh, such young hands, to be in.

Another new drug? my mouth says.
Will it give me bloat, sloth, both?
it cannot say.
Thoughts are four quintuplets.

He plays with a slow hand.
Looks straight up.
Then rifles rock staccato.
We're done for today,
                    two thumbs somehow say.

The Stone In My Shoe

I cheer every tragedy
I read about. I nod
when I hear of cliff
plunges or death
on the tracks:
suicide never lets me go.
I walk with its stone in my shoe.

Suicide is not ex nihilo.
I live this one life
condemned on death row.
This short history of decay
lingers. Death fascinates.
Drugs delay. Fluxotine,
lithium, loxapine,
stigmata, Abilify, alcohol.

It grips my right hand
often, pressing blunt
knives and rusted razors
into a sleeve of pretty
pink and white scars.
The language of this limbo.

But one day I'll be pushed.
To permanence.

                        To suffer no more.

My Fingers Shake

> The vineyard sheep bleat
> across the village. From one side to the other,
loud then quiet, like a nineties rock song.
They take turns to call. They've not wasted billions
of years evolving speech.

> From my balcony, my call back
> is hard toffee—
cracking teeth and gumming up gums
as it mangles words and strangles languages.

I find a needle and red thread
in the drawer, beside toothpicks and two balls
of twine. I hold this mouth of mine,
pierce the top lip—first.

> I leave room for air
to expire, but not so much for even an *i*
to escape. I shake my fleece,
finger letters, and spin my words
for yarn after yarn.

The Idiot's Guide To Suicide

Speak to someone.
Everything's going to be OK.
Everyone gets down.
It's just a bad mood.
Life's a gift.
But get a grip.
Be mindful.
There's an app for that.

Let's tackle the stigma:
go to bed early.
Slow down—
Or, if you can't, run, run, run.
Breathe properly.
Keep a happy diary.
Lower your aims.
And hide your arms.

Walk into the light.
It's OK not to be OK.
You're bent not broken.
Happiness is a choice.
Live in the actual moment.
Life is about starting over—
one breath at a time.
You need to try yoga.

Things could be worse.
Cuddle your pet.
Take out the rubbish.
Do some colouring in.
And cover your arms.
Take a warm bath.
Be kind to yourself.
Spend time in nature.

        You're a caterpillar.
You can be the butterfly.

Down
the
road,
      not across the street.

The Silent Echoes Of Prangins

A man stares up at me, comes
up to me. Wears every

yesterday on the soles of his shoes.
Tomorrow already hollows

his bones. He glares
with defused cannon eyes.

Atones. He's been dumb
for six months.

A mind quarantined
from the body. Their victory over

him—over mystery—ends
only when the balloon

man comes. Words gripped
together with strips

of masking tape.
Letters fall

as unseen crumbs
swell in the sink.

He shouts
sentences as short as summer.

14

He's been deep, vessels hard
to reach, crack always to gorm

less. Folds drag and decay.
Grattez un peu grattez ma peau.

The skin stinks, stinks of truth,
Peels his *peau* all summer long

long strips of *craiceann*[1] crackle
and buckle. The sun grains

scorch, shrivel—leave him
to screeve, die, and lie

outside the high wall.
His task in the future
no one knows.

---

[1] *Irish word for skin*

TV Fault Finding

Backs off wood TVs
innards laid out
on fairway-deep flax.
Peered-over thick glasses.
Graphene-thin, steady fingers
bulbous valves,
even then looking like museum pieces
future fittings for barber shops.

Valves in the shed
valves in the sitting room
valves all over the family car.

I never saw the face in that TV frame.
I prayed for tubes to seize and shatter.
Now it doesn't much matter.
Loose keys and thrown knees,
a yellow-tinged ghostly outline.

The Box

I pick up a grey fluffy jumper
from the bathroom floor.

It's got one more wear in it
then it's no longer you.

I put it in the box
with the scarlet-haired Barbie

the pink microphone stand
that biting tiger fish

a suctioned-out baby
self-scar-faced walker

eight-year-old laugher
my one dreamed daughter.

Hold them tight in lined hands
gently place them in the box.

In the box. Here no more.
In the box. I'll never stop

carrying that box
on sloping shoulders

Oh, I've missed you all the while
my darling little child

the box will never fill with dresses
and places that carry you away.

I keep on, I carry the box
I fill the box with years and tears

the good kind too
the ones that make you heave,

pulling every muscle
into your life's one smile.

The Cycle

I am getting used to the tumble
the low bass rumble in my head.
The growing grumble from outside.
All will come out in the cycle.

To have no control
to feel fresh but completely used.
to be tossed in the slotter
in clothes and clutter. Agitated.

I'm pulled out when the ups stop.
The cycle continues. I'm dragged
out, prodded, wrung, hung out
to drip dry. Scrub and scrape

say the white coats, do not leave
a mark. I'm bundled
into a top-down dryer barrel
spun for fun. I have the mark.

He is unclean, they say.
My incense of fragrant drugs
says I am unclean, nods
in the street say I'm unclean.

What proceeds out the brain
is what defiles the man.
I am washed, backwashed,
spun, swash, double dried.

Those who are clean don't need
a doctor. He does not heal
the righteous, but sinners.
The mark persists

in the warp or in the woof.
Wash me again, stretch me
on the rack, the washboard
beat me

with your battledore,
scour me on metal
feed me to the one-way
wringer.

Never stop folding
me. I never thought
I'd live to escape
the cycle.

Every Breath Is Like The First

Can you dream me now?
Days since you opened your eyes.
Every life is like the first,
guess right, find where your north lies,
but I see your first cells' course.

Your thoughts haunt all I can't want; false fuse lit.
Life fades when that fire blunts, and the shit hits.
Yahweh brought more worlds and atoms split,
to free us and spin new spheres to tilt.

Mo chroi, taunt as much as you want, but I'm Gaunt.
I've love just enough to gift you my second-best blanket.
One-night stand and my tears can't betray.
Don't cry, tighten pink fists, oversoon infant.

Are you free of me now?
Prised that cord from the sore skies?
Every breath is like the first.
You feel fate right now
The fight/fright of our unmoored lives.
As I hear your last cell divide.

One Life Later

No one has the self-same mother, siblings
most of all.
　　　Your brother gets way more
time on his console than you
and you wear more hand-me-downs
than him.
　　　You're in different hemispheres:
in one he smiles,
in the other she frowns. When
　　　you, again,
scrape Teflon from a pan,
　　　your mile-a-minute mind
whispers that she loves him more.
And she does.
　　　You exist in a tiny world which all ignore.
Crying curled in the bottom
bunk, mix of girl and clotted gore.
　　　One life later,
　　　you are plain to pearl.
　　　Your child
is nature, your favourite flavour. Her
raven curls are yours, her beam teaches
you to smile.
　　　You remain each other,
not just for nine months, but for
lives.
　　　You are no longer
squashed bug on a windowpane
but a trilling triumph who flies
with stained glass wings.

Never Let Go

When we were stung,
you held me,
(a little too tightly)
and hummed along
to the songs on the radio.
And never let go.

When I was numb,
I etched into my skin,
(a little too sharply).
I plunged headlong,
and watched the rust red flow:
faster, then slow.

Kneeblades

My kneeblades are a Gilla Band track.
I crave a quack's crack. Cure

as attack. I cry driving home
through the chicanes. Bone brillos

bone. Now it never stops. Nerves
betray. Find their own frequency

of suffering. I hid behind surreal.
Now I'm nothing but real.

Why have I blades where I once
had knees? My legs rotate on a skewer

after the death disco. I push
blue crystal cold packs right

onto my skin. I fuck off the pain.
I hear bone drilling is real.

Patella meet femur. My marriage profane.
This song is a bone cleaver.

This chorus is desolation fever.
Crack me, break me, remake

me. Post bail free. Bones make
me. Set pain free. These death legs

go on shaking.

Shards Much Sharper Than The Others

You sprint to nowhere.
I fall up your weaves
to a place we have been
hundreds of times
Your post-midnight blue hair
shimmers in the blizzard.
I cloak back
to where I died,
was sanctioned, and sectioned.

The four-storey four-century house
dazzles in the storm
like that brown box smile's
fever dream.
Does it matter that you'd kept me waiting
inside the world's smallest waiting room?

All day long,
I explain in bad French
that tremors do not travel.
Stuck in a snow globe
shaken and sheened with salt
Pac-Man trapped
in one screen, force-fed
power pills.

You make me wait
eleven more hours
threaten to keep me
in. But you deliver
Temesta. The best, yeah!
And tell me not to take it
until the morning after the drive home.

I don't, so I don't kill a broken fox
pulling one paw in front of the other
on the route de Genève.
The next morning
I take it. Embrace it.
I smear myself all down
the curve of the parking lot.
Shards jag red.
Paint.
This time.

Phoebe Bridgers

I've had more shrinks than lovers.
That sounds like Phoebe Bridgers.
But she mines thunder tattoos
for sacred scriptures.

Her lookalike stands on carved
curated legs in the waiting room.
Ink swirls from under her skin
and bears witness. A flock escapes
a cage on an upper arm, a thigh
is the canvas for a lightning bolt
striking a pictogram girl.

We're all waiting for therapy,
she's in for more than me.
Her teenage son's glasses blend
with a phone screen before
they're marched off
by the mother's image
negative.

I'm dumped by another therapist
—it's not him, it's me, and I spot
the etched woman at reception.
We walk out together but alone.

Electric Dreams

I'm strapped down in a locked-down
Lausanne hospital. The relaxant
readies my body. A tiny bell
rings as I go under. A hand
fixes wet metal electrodes.

     I am gone

and seize and spasm.
The god Lugh stands seven foot
above me, hair the colour of pooled
blood. His spear surges
through my brain.
I come round with a smile
that attains my ears, a fleeting
feat, and devour the world's
silkiest vanilla yoghurt.

Nine times that bell chimes.
Nine times, lightning strikes.
Nine times, a mind cracks.

Cherish

The clatter comes first. The smack.
A grown man with too styled
too long silver hair swings
his grown man fist
into the side of my twelve-year-old head.
My stupid ear stings.
My stupid world rings.
My teeth feel all wrong.

My tongue lolls, my eyes widen
to skies. I'm a cow.
He pulls the next punch
cuffs my nose.
I am wet. Snot.

The Proclamation[2] roared:
Cherish all children
of the nation
Equally. In misery.

But no child was cherished here
between nineteen sixteen.
and nineteen ninety-two.

Equal to freeze in inside outhouses.
Equal to disappear in big houses,
on streets that look away.
Equal to drown in uncovered pits,

---

[2] *Proclamation of 1916 Easter Rising*

Handprints on my back. A holy show.
How many slaps today?
the 'oul ones ask at the avenue gates at three fifteen.
Just my ear pulled. Just my hair yanked
to the corner. With me following.
Just my stutter laughed at
by the master
then the boys
stiffly smiling, happy
it's not them.

The boys and girls
                in their mortal care,
the boys and girls
                who were never there,
the boys and girls
                who never were.

ii

the universe

Divine Projection

The universe shrinks to smaller pieces
as it expands. Once, we were made of stars.
Now, we're bodies of atoms, or neutrons,
or tiny non-cheese quarks. Just how many
leptons are in a soul anyway?
Are all the neutrinos in each
universe going to heaven?

Why stare at a shepherd's delight sunset,
or into a child's eyes or at Hubble
shots— flickers of the furthest away star?
We anthropomorphise ants and gods. Seek
prisms in the sky, scribble, and scratch
on standing stones. Build bigger
colliders so they will come. We take
the divine from all we that we spy and touch.

Mindless
Of having put it there
in the first place.

I See Black

In a river of twisted time,
we inhabit a narrow fold of space.

The wails of terrified new-borns,
learning the world
is larger than us.

The black and purple, murk
and must of Catholicism—
perfectly packaged fear. I spent
my teens kneeling—and then repenting.
The fear of failure, the daily dirge
of labour.

I can go to the street
and have pistachio ice-cream, read
five lines, or reach to touch a freckled arm.
But I roll and roll my ball of dung.
My eye takes in a thousand shades of light,
but I see black.

Lost

I can't get lost when it's so quiet
in here. They say it's not going
to help that we're all at each other's throats.
But I try to transport myself. Imagine
I'm an albatross soaring alone

in a private
sky.

No need to chart a course.
A mollymawk above the mere meer,
I circle the globe and never feel
solid ground. No watching clock,
no finical flock— alone, unbound.

One

I did not come greedy gilled
from the sea. Neither am I
simian sprung. I am not druid
or believer. Not native or invader.

Nineteen-sixteen is not me.
I am neither war nor peace,
not north or south. I seek
no mother, brother, lover. Not
Fein, Fail, or Fine.

Or ally or activist. I float
adrift from any family
tree. My tongue is not
scarred by language. I do
not find shelter in others.

I have no nation
or destination.

I will not become
dust or ash
or clay.

The Crab

The word was never said in our house,
only when the horoscopes were read out:
your own judgment is most important,
your peers admire your choices.
Or, when neighbours visited, and I was banished
from the sitting room—where I'd be sat
on the springy russet sofa watching snooker on *Grandstand*—
to the dim dining room,
where I'd earwig and hear,
through the hollow core door,
Mrs Coyle mouth the word:
Did you hear that Red Pat has it?—
riddled with it, the poor cratur.

Grown now, cameras are pushed into me,
searching for that crab nebula
and finding it, late stage and aggressive.
I'm now scared, scarred, and unable to pee.
They cut away cells, cells, and dignity
and, still, I cannot say its name.

The Jewel Sting

The wheel gets harder to turn.
My flesh is his and his only.
I found out at fifteen immersed
in his dark. His slaps stung,
his words more, his brutish body
tore. I still smell his *Joop!*, for God's sake,
and decay. I thought I'd blocked it
out from myself.

      So what now?

Existence slithers like a sequence
of unease. All I feel, recoil from,
is designed—to displease.
Every life is a time-bound moment,
escape attempts as futile
as those of the cockroach,
controlled by a jewel wasp sting.

The Trials of Tutankhamun

The candle lights the crowbar. Fat fingers pick
at everything. Jars, jasper, beetle wings.
Royal foetuses, nightshade berries. Plunder
and science are never satisfied. They slide
beneath bandages. Every grasper
disturbs Tut's bed. His eyes do not blink.
We weigh not just hearts but heads.
Almond eyes and stripling's skin profaned
by three dee autopsies. Every drab age
focuses its glare to miss what once dazzled.

iii

the universe and other people

Epic

I throw you
two and then three cushions
for you to build a wall,
then a room,
then a tomb,
for when our boy returns.
You called him Jon
because he was only half-human,
and you stalked each other
all his six thousand days.

You extract the cups from the
dishwasher with needless crashes
and caroms; you only communicate
in cacophony, smash a painted robin
cup, perching cocky no more.

Those tumbler spalls assail
my stockinged feet.
You don't hoover and I'm desultory.
Every hour stills my heart
I'm jabbed; you've let the fever
in. You burrow into a chair,
upholstered like a 1990s tie,
the one we weaned Jon on.
Now, you rave directions
from or to the grim reaper.

It wasn't the first time
that he disappeared. Hardly
a vanishing act though; it's
always a lake, or a train track,
or a hotel.

Negative life never let him go—
it wanted a world without him. That pull
was too strong.
No chats, pills, talking
or non-talking therapists,
suicide watches, or performative
marches were going to save him.

He was relentless.
He had the balls to walk his dark path.
I put his things aside—that Zlatan shirt,
his boxing gloves, the mouse he knitted—
but he was never here.
He and you are bones and torment,
and, in six hundred days,
I will put your things aside too.

Sunny Side Up

—after Michael Hofmann

I could compute the cosmic odds that pulled
protons, electrons, and neutrons
in just the right configuration,
the proper path for you and me.

I could praise the Lord, the one Creator
who let there be light, made heaven
and earth, visible and invisible,
forged us from dust.

I could become the James Webb
Telescope to see ancient stars forming,
to travel back billions of years, to see
the invisible engineer at work.

I could quibble with Darwin
on survival of the weakest,
but thank the primate pilots who rafted
over oceans. No monkeys, no apes, no us.

I could thank creator, engineer, chance
for the miracle of you. For firing
the flame of your hair, of your will. For
forgiving me, setting me free.

I could be the man with two faces.
Living life with no fear. I could see
choices and know there's a way. For you
and me, no matter what they say.

Fate and faith and cosmic circumstance
worked their science and sorcery.
To bring your dreams and dust to me.
But my heart falls heavy. All that
effort for me—and you, I guess—
and you could just as easily
have hatched from an egg.
And, still, I'd desire and devour you—
poached, scrambled, or sunny side up.

On Weather

I was the ferocity of a summer day
You, constant as the gulf stream,
supplanting frigidity with balm.

Me, a gentle breeze on your neck,
a first snowflake melting on the road.
You, the equator and all the tropics,
bulging but always in the right place.

I floated a cumulus adrift,
you pulled the tides, as told by the moon.
I was waving—and drowning.
You at sea level, impervious.

I was weather, and you were climate:
changeless, even in this Gretan age.

The Man Who Knew Exactly When To Leave

We cross on the playground's red paving.
He gestures hello and beckons
down at his black cumbrous
walker, raising his eyes at the same time.
I scrape out a sentence in French,
that the withering sun
has wiped out his beloved garden.
After the suffering, the rain, he says.

He is no more, she whispers loudly
in the no-man's land echo inside
the red lift, voice caught like mud on
a dog. Her wavering pitch shift
is a kissed frog. She means he is dead,
the next-door neighbour. I rushed
to hug but wanted to bite and
bruise to taste that tough tamarack

skin, to catch and avoid those soft
eyes, to watch him stoop with cool coins
to make the tough kids cry. The black
and brown leather jacket swings on the back
of the door, mocking his gibbet.
His tatted wings. His cork door wreath
is not here. His white bin bag is
not here.

Found

She allowed me to go,
but I never arrived.
I had fire in my belly,
I went door to door,
to every club in the city.
And I found my heart spilled
on the night I was killed.

I was found naked—
in just a teddy boy
coat—in the meeting
house lane. They came
in fours or fives, the blue girls,
and stared and shrugged.
On the morning I was found.

Propped up,
among the dock leaves
lining the cobble stones,
I watched them prod
and photo me. Saw
them look past me.
On the morning I was found.

I'm shining in the sun.
Before—I'd hide in the flat
or, if she sent me out,
I'd blink and squint,

and girls would heckle
at my shorts and freckles.
In the summer, she prowled.

"Party boy found dead"—
"Nude and assaulted".
No one saw, no one spotted.
Y-cut, waked, satin cushion,
in my only suit in a pine coffin.
Only magpies mourn.
When I am fed,
to the ground.

Distortion

I distorted you, contorted you,
saw through your sunshine.
Astounded you, confounded you,
the vinegar to your fine wine.
Exhorted you and extorted you,
made you trek my steep incline.
Tried to fight you and spite you,
but worshipped at your shrine.

Then we met, that darkest night,
you wouldn't come to mine.
You disowned me, wouldn't phone me,
left me suppliant and supine.
Now you shame me and reclaim me,
cure me with your brine.
You have tamed me, even lamed me,
carved a new man from my spine.
You have smited me and righted me,
spun me back to normal time.

Your freckles guide me, red hair hides me,
your touch calms my manic mind.
But you uncoil me and deploy me,
then manage my decline.
You watch me destroy me,
as I ripen profane not divine.
My bones walk, my soul stalks—you—
until the end of time.

The Gazed Girl In The Manhattan Window

Every hour is a Tuesday
evening. I kill every second
but they keep on coming.
There's a dream
to being in love.
A gaze, a window

a face formed and noble
perfectly oval
colour long
bleached out. A gaze, a face
not for fitted Fair Isle jumpers

or crop tops. A gaze for an era
that will never be.
My own
pale gaze happens
to make you
out in the reflection of a Manhattan

street. Who are you? When
are you? Those viaduct brows
above eyes piercing
every moment,
Cupid on your left cheek
searches for his bow in a triangle
of doubtless mouth.

Grumma of gas lights, everybody
runs, low scooters dodge a baseball
-capped burnt sienna six-oh-five.
Still you stare. Returning
to where?
There's a dream to being alive.

Slow Dance

Clam cold hand on small of my back
his shirt washing powder-ad white
no forcing touch or moment,
a second:
> of everything being right
> kiss
> bite

My flame, hair tumbles,
my left arm, his neck, fumbles
the floor is hardwood, dark
soft and light beneath us
his hair so dark it reflects
every disco light
smells fresher than any baby
teeth touched, lips locked,
docked, soon rovers.

The slow song slows
its final note
I retreat on toes,
closed throat, shed troth

> dropped rose.

Eva

She sits with her hands
adrift, hovering over her lap.

Her limbs were feet, in size
and shape...but in texture, consistency,

a nest of twigs. Her carmine dress,
creased in all the wrong

places, looks fashioned
for another body

or species. Her beauty
can't be of this world,

only detectable
in the shy sway of her

orbit. Or etched olive
on her face, as on canvas,

masked by layers and layers
of mottled and speckled

paint, only visible from
the just-so angle, under

the right light—in rare
moods. She is cursed

with the gift of finding
the pain of others.

Now faceless, tottering,
the highwire walker
falls.

Sunday Morning Petit-Lancy Tea-room

My voices are silent.
The soft esses and pauses
of native tongues.
I reach to catch every third word.
Chinoise, couteau, cinema.
Cutlery is clattered
silence never there
shattered. Three men
with shared dark tight hair
shared Balkan tongue
coo over three-month-old gurgles.
Babble. A silent pair in lagging jackets
nurse two defiant beers
seconds silently ticking 'til noon.
I extend two *renversés* to one
sipping hour. The low hum
enfolds and insulates against
the Petit-Lancy chill
which whistles in the still.

Silk Strings

I can't see the silk strings
but my limbs feel your touch.

With a twitch of movement
I come to life.

I open in each wrist,
each knee, my back

below. I'm hooked in the holed
head. You brush my cold

porcelain, run your fingers
into me, cracked cockroaches,

mouse's blood. You caress
my woven head, stuffed

with folded memories
of moonless nights

when you would come
for me. *Dalang*, heed no censor,

play me for your yearning tune.
I will cleave and contort

to dance a cotillion for you.

58

Right in Two

I've done the maths enough to know
that you are the square
root of me, from high to low,
plus and minus.

Nested variables, our equations
unworkable
you know my unknowns; our divisions
multiply.

A pair of unequal equations,
abacus beads,
locked forever on distant rods
for gods to solve.

First and Knew

We first found each other
in the glances of others.

I tangled myself in red
vines. Dot to dotted freckles

of her. Figured out her French,
every language she didn't speak.

She's the city, she's the sea
the reflection in every eye.

They wear black ties, tight suits,
stubble's badly erased blackboards.

They sit on the new red throw
on the sticky black sofa,

my thirty-three years being borne,
let down again, buried

with every gut instinct,
four thousand bad decisions.

For she is here, I am born.
I would happily die

for her. But she doesn't yet exist.
The thrushes are singing

Wichita lines are ringing.
Around men long enough

she hides her own grace.
But her message is sent

sticks in me like a stent.
Her glance the urgency

in every instant.

The Reflection

I appear in every glass
the centre of the world, the circumference also.
I am every reflection
in bathrooms
behind bars through tinted train tunnels

Scarring everyone I've ever met,
thought about, minded,
all who have breathed
my name, took it in vain.

I'm Borges' abomination,
multiplying me and universes
carried along. I stand
in a thousand places at once.
Fear stoked, doubt seeded.
When you check
your hair in the rear-view mirror,
that's me you see.
So wonder not why
I'm here, or guess how, but ask where
I'm taking you, and how far.

He Leads Us into the Depths

I've just seen Nick Cave.
In Montreux. He is the vampire
king but his feral symphonies
are drowned by the rattles
of pearls from balconies.
There are no spirits
or sparks in Montreux town.
Every thought and deed is billed on
green paper and noted
in black books.

I thought Switzerland was cold, he says,
and leads us from this steam
chamber. We follow with the mad
rooks, past the food
and bible stalls
into the bubbling Lac Léman.
The thin dark spook
screams and the thin dark spook
shouts. The slicked back hair
falls lose as he sneers
and spits.

He parts the lake
all the way
to Evian's orange
lights. The waves are walls.
Bankers and traders

and watchers drown
until they're dead.
Moneychangers and prospectors
too. Little fish eat
through their heads.

But we and he, his deep
blue suit wicking
every drop, walk and wade
through the deep. Up
the thousand steps. Up
to the long black train,
sixty coaches long. No
more pain and suffering.
That train of hope
and intent, where cash
and souls
are never spent.

iv

beast of burden

Ibex Cry

Ibex horns are too long.
I spot one sometimes
in summer valleys—
its dunnish coat makes it more deer
than goat—when the ski gondolas
have long stopped and everything
is white and pink. In reality, he spots
me and is watchful and wary
as if he alone must stop
his kind from being wiped out
again. I move closer, and tell him
that I don't want his flesh or his hide.

I am now close
enough to count
rings at the back of his horns.
As well as mobile medicine chest
he is a tree on four legs. I think
of drinking from those magnificent
horns and I'm pretty sure they wouldn't
detect poison in my parting
glass. But I can crush them
down to a powder, like
the snow, to cure
my hysterics. If I didn't
have toes for fingers, I'd carve
the rest into that snuff
box I've always needed.

His stony existence
will be the cure for the stones
in my bladder, my kidneys, in my head.
Next, I will drink—and why not
use the horns as cups—the warmth
the delicate clot texture, the forbidden?
Now, I am clean,
I am free
I am a god who will
feast on the ibex cry for centuries.

Sixty-seven Storks

Sixty-seven storks came
before you were born,
the *cigognes* of Aubonne.
One nested on our roof.
My name's 23, she said.
She was huge, six feet or more
from tail to beak, wing to wing.
Her feathers were the kind of white
that contained every colour.
Her wing tips were ink black
like the mother of all birds.

She cocked her head to speak,
a clash, crack and clattering
of the long red swords: her beak.
In a mix of machine gun
and morse, she said she'd bring a boy
in winter, now that she didn't stay
in Africa, but in the
full landfills of Spain.

The boy will have red plumage,
with dots on a face of frost.
Our own faces were touching,
my body stretching out of my roof's skylight
with 23's bill poking in,
scouring for moles and voles.
I'm not even peckish,

she said, reading my mind,
your lizards are to die for.
He'll be soft and so strong
and not often wrong.

She retreated her beak.
a soft touch of wing on bill
to say her goodbye—
but stopped as coolly as she flew
and said—*oh, by the nests,*
later there will be a girl,
dogged and half horse, half human.
This time she did retreat—
gracefully of course—
but not before one last clonk:
When the time comes, I'll carry them
over rising seas and
wild forests to find heaven
in the too-hot human hell.

Duel and Dance

The hawks are duelling.
As they shear the sky, they play not prey.
They are kites.

Black silhouetted.
They weave inside and out of their own
joint orbits

like wily winger
and aged wary fullback. They swoop
and they soar.

Unfettered
by mere three dimensions, their talons
tangled,

they spiral, saccade
towards the deep azure below.
Prey, beware.

Bright in the Daygloom

The egret is bright in daygloom
strutting its flat field domain
much more stridently
than on my favourite
album cover.
Grubs and scurrying ghosts
dot its keen sight lines,
yellow feather fringed eyes
like cue balls after
black chalk shots
nail every pot.

The Murder of Crows

Black-suited, black-hatted men,
coattails flapping, on all-black bikes—
no helmets, gears, gear, lanes.
Septuagenarians, they sweep
along boreens like grass in the gravel.
At dusk they silhouette the sky—
riding, roding woodcocks. Now
new elastane peacocks preen,
these cocks and crows are dodos.

Murmurs

The murmuration has split and escaped.
The windows rattle in the western wind;
badgers and stoats scatter, snouts flared—this plague
purges beasts, closes throats; our torments twinned.

         The bird boy is here as I nurse my cup,
           Dark, bitter, reviving, a ritual.
He says he has a fresh hex to fix up, his blackthorn eyes
               are through me
              —filial and fierce.

Now   you   will   write,   your   word   or   God's,
but for Them, and Approval. And each rhyme
will   keen   my   short   time.
I   could   only   nod.
Was happy to, I clasped his \hand/ this time.

We murmur farewells, I stroke his oil-spilled coat,
and he rises with a whirr and a whistle,

and is

—

gone.

v

i will be the stone

Women of No Property

I crack
and they see all the darkness in me.
I am a silhouette flickering on the wall.
They weave my warrant from tears
and tattooed threats.

The air is a syrup of souls.
This world is stained orange and black.
Aflame drumlins hide blood oaths.

I undermine
the stability of society.
I scribble sedition.
I waste paper.
So now I drink dirty water
in a red blood cell—
and must put Tone and Griffith,
Larkin and Davitt, and Connolly
and Casement in the wrong order.

We're shuffling mummies,
every face bandaged.
The first were taken
to this half-built hotel

in the night.

Now the people
are dragged two by two
by the guards

in broad day gloom.

Sometimes, the undead
make it this far.

Believe

—after Shu Ting and Faith No More

Nineties boys can't face the truth. Like spears
they still believe.

We want it all and we can't have it.
It's in your hands and you can't grasp it.

Now your slate suit trousers ride up,
your head is held back.

Your undelivered future waits,
she rubs her hands together as she shields

the sun of another hottest day.
You break free and totter

over ten thousand broken tents to reach
the city city's port; unseeing upside-down dinghies

on the horizon. The mourning after.
We all partied. Body folded

in three, hands grip the ground,
mouth already fallen in disgust:

No one is left behind
No one excluded
We're the people who get up early.

You sit on the ground cradling
your knees, bare slabs, barer

toes, upturned head, swept black
mane, ringed eyes seeking stars.

Everything
you believed is dead.

I Will Be the Stone

Great heists were
performed by master
magpies pickpocketing paintings
and stealing gold and glisten.
Condensed wealth redistributed.
But even the trickiest tea leafs
cannot grab city skylines for their swag
bags. Now all that glisters is glass. Wealth
of a nation, many nations. The celestial
cities gleam like none before, so laundered
and washed. We chumps, in awe, must drag
ourselves away from society squandered.
Oligarchy, kleptocracy, the ruin of billions
for the wants of few. I will be the first stone,
but you're the slingshot.

Crash. Smash. Thrash.

Backlash.

Uncache cash.

Soon, we will dance on
shards of glass to the death of debt. From Dubai
to Dublin, we will tear their shelters down, sunder
their plunder, crush their unearned authority.
Pane by painful pane.

The Tenant

My tenancy ran out
months ago but I'm still wedged
here. I couldn't pay so they hung me
up on the wall in my flat
that's now an investment.

The glass frame hides my splayed
shame, not the orange fire
of it. I'll be bought and sold
again. Moulded into something
more functional.

Southsiders love a puffer jacket
and the scally in it
wrapped around their boilers.
Human defaulter driers are as popular
as refugee draft excluders.

You, your family
your contour
leg pillow
your ceiling
your hybrid
are all owned.
Time ticks on rental
and mental states:
the process of the workers'
obsolescence has begun.

Just abide by the terms
of your lease
your release,
and your cease-breeding-and-desist.
You are the die in the game
that only the *others* play.

[the amazon started as a stream]

the amazon started as a stream
but can now reach loutish space
hail the self-enskying bullshit bond villain
the all-time king of the dudes.

watching the wrong brothers take flight
like schoolboys chasing a cherry
to pop; lust coming to the brim
as fanboys queue to rim.

back on the earth aflame, I scream:
humans, we have a problem
as an app pings in my palm
and I'm sacked for walking out.

who needs a freshly-fired picker?
I start again, in my prime
zero hours are better than none.
now your driver, I pee as I go.

I tumble home after 15 hours
the tv's flickers fill the room
I keep the volume way down
so as not to wake my parents.

I get rudely awakened by that spaceman
I put my trousers on
and I think about buying a house
and sob when my giggles stop.

I am back in orbit by 8AM
handling a van too big
for a body which is now mostly ribs
as I stretch shifts to empty hours.

I can outdo roger bannister
and deliver in four minutes
if I leave the seat-belt loose
and drop at your door.

the space oddity returns
the hardest thing is stopping him imprint
a cuddled CEO can come to think
of itself as human.

Shared Delusion

—after Bjørge Lillelien

They haunt shops, beam
from scrubbed screens.
Crisp or crinkled, they stamp on hearts,
leech on the clotted stream.

He's a ten but his tales are too gritty.
In hard times, there are no expectations,
great or otherwise. Paper forged, even eaten.
Want needs, greed feeds.

She sighs as I unfold her.
A hazel lady's life on canvas.
No queen or colleen, she's all of us,
Erin's image, keening for Collins.

Oh, my country, my flag, golden
sun of May. They try to sink you—
but you watermark every note.
No cowry, just what folds.

Dickens, Lady Lavery, Manuel Belgrano,
Banjo Patterson, Frank Worrell, Apiaguaiki Tumpa,
Greta Garbo, you have beaten us all,
beaten us all.

Nikola Tesla, can you hear me?
Can you hear me, Nikola Tesla?
Presses keep on printing,
but where's our glinting gold?

The famous as flesh made paper.
Proxies for the placenta
that feeds greed and condemns
all of us to wage labour.

All of them were there, paper
ghosts. Used and abused,
for coins and notes,
of no worth, no value.
                    *
The shared delusion,
you are what you pay
in this life, when money,
like the Tonlé Sap, only trickles
up.

Ireland 2023

The final saint—and scholar—on this distraint isle.
They built your house so that it would crumble.
The GPO is fallen
GDP is rising.
Our fallen in tents freezing,
one rough sleeper in a poncho wheezing,
brawls with a broken boy from a better land,
for the circling vultures
riotous and redheaded
—maddened by mammon's call—
screech and shout:
'*Look after our own first!*'
and '*Get a job, you junkie scum!*'
Cranes sway the sky,
concocting symmetrical squares of supply.
Not the homes or even houses we demand,
but deposit boxes, all the same.
For men were born to prey and save
and grasp their killings in the grave.

Elegy for an Empire

—after Alfred Tennyson

Call off the search. There is no state
of wonder and certainty. Skies
are gunmetal grey and I am
in black leather.

Seconds later
the morning sun shines far too fierce.
Its death rays pierce all protection.
Today I eye roll scoff at solemn
mourning. The world is black and
pangs. Their queen reigns no more.

      Everywhere

fawning doffing and, yes, taunting.
Everyone's granny is the final empress.

Ours are shouts of heathens and traitors.
Tweets, insults, filth, and monstrous testimonies.
The void consumes all. Say what we say are the
groans of the living, and voices of the dead.

This is not the time for broken bodies,
shot children, African chains, pre-paid metres,
plunder. This is a safe space for just
one suffering. Silence follows this pure death.

Heirs sleep peaceably in their beds
because enough men stand ready to stay silent.
The hush palls but when the waterless day
grows drier, before hindsight's falling, comes

a bitter stink, down from the south. It blows
our rest aside and with that stench, the tide
rises as if each creature in the kingdom
had also passed simultaneously

their very motions and rose this spoor smirr.
With less and less we vanish into night.
Our putrefaction and death pyres offend.
The new son rises, but this king holds his nose.

Checkpoints

The soldier, pimpled, younger than his helmet
eyes twitching to every movement
a retriever sensing a treat
rifles through the boot of my dad's
sky-blue Opel Kadett estate,
its bounty of broken TVs,
their spilled innards of bulbous valves
betraying wires.

The squaddie watches the suspect,
who trembles from the same fear
that makes the gun shake.

Back in his parent's house in Toxteth or Easington,
he hides, from them,
from border memories.
Contrition nags,
like my dad knocking
on the moss green shed door
where I'm not there.

Dawns Are Different

My skin is ashen.
I spend my days doing laundry.
I burn, I vomit.

I know it is a Sunday
because they hold a rally
every Sunday.

I miss the theatre.
They stroke my hair
and pluck them.

The president's left;
it's like a new perfume
I burn, I vomit.

I worked quickly,
tasting time.
I wake up tired,
fired

lying
on the side of the road.
They eat people like ghosts.
I burn, I vomit.

vi

things falling apart

Unspecified Environmental Disaster II

Stuck in the middle, it
moves faster than me. Light;

life. Snow, scree, the
quondam mountain

skis. We pump shots;
hit what we need to

hit. The drop from
the top is too steep.

The cascade shears
the peak. Water has no

froth or flow. Silver
strands pleach. The stream

founders. The valley
too. The whole hill

sunders. Green and white
now steeped in muck turns

brown and boulder grey.
Small men hare here, there

but no
where.
No one
is coming

to save us now.

Things Falling Apart

No order in chaos, just chaos.
You cannot and do not resist—just as
the great prairie chicken cannot
stop dancing, moaning, and flashing
his lifejacket neck every spring.

The world's piggy bank tilts
further towards the moneyed:
your cosy climate crashes;
you throttle coalmine canaries.
The end
of an error means more
terror.
Life is designed—
by a god or bored coder—
to lose order.

Stop tilting at waterfalls. You don't need
answers, just better questions.
It makes sense that today is more
complex than when your favourite band
was killing you.
Let the currents of chaos
overwhelm you.
Embrace it, ordain it.

Or—forsake it.
Be Dali. Melt time to create order.
Be Marty.   Go forward to the past.
But you will wait.
Not long now
until your bones buckle and reason fails—
things fall apart, that's all.

Viscous

The day is inside a jam jar.
The air is treacle:
it bungs and clogs lungs
in black tar. A haunted hawk
halts, its fat feathers gummed
in the soaring slot as if
by Exxon-Valdez crude.

Below, human sun basters
stew. A boutique hotel's
brown brick and brunches
in aspic. Melting mouths suck
never chew. Lava steams up
car windows without love
or lust. On gossamer skin
boils blister and blisters
boil. The world dozes,
one leg dangling
from its duvet.

Die or Pause

Three faded women wandered,
bit by bit, across the bitumen.
Here is your lot, one shouts as I pass.
Sleek SUVs, boxy sports cars, each a lane
and a half in acreage, go nowhere.

Instead, dead drivers and cars stranded,
a deleted scene from a Radiohead
video. Humans jilted by metal
myrmidons. Here and no further.

Said Christine and Christine. Here,
heads are slivered by exploded airbags,
their throats throttled by seatbelts.
The undeclared war now has a foe

or folly. Further on, cars are overgrown
by towering grass, humans too. Fossilised
fools. Concrete cracks, tar slithers
back to the core. We will drive

no more, the drives dictate; later planes
and pipelines too mandate. I wander lonely
in that crowd. Those still breathing slump.
Then slow, stop, and sink.

Bright orange butterflies swarm
insensate on sacred firs.

Pest

I perform ever grander gestures; still fail to rouse you.
I turn the leaves later every autumn,
from green to dull custard in weeks.
No need for my Titian palette or shades
of amber, but you will not heed. Your seas
swell, your peaks melt. Fingers in ears,
no fears or tears, poked-out eyes will not see.

Endless hot wars will kill, but you say, *not here*.
A trillion cows belch and your frail lungs fail.
It's not the ice caps or port cities that will fall,
but your stretch, your flesh, your reign.
I live—my trees and seas safe from treaties,
and the human need to grow and conquer.
Farewell my best pest—next time, stay longer.

Hear the Meek Yell

We are with the worms, squelched in
the maundering mud. Under a
milk micro moon. Toes are chilled
and blained

fingers fail to fit undarned
gloves. Soon the majestic morning will
herald the final wake. Already
these plots smell. All scars

unheal. Our souls' senses now quickening
—are they not? The mad are now
sane, bones are not our own.
Hear the meek yell, I don't believe

the lies you tell. But coffins creak.
Our blood boils. Our lungs clogged.
Paradise is spoiled. We believe that we meant
well. Before turning heaven into
this aguey hell.

The Roar

Four fat bees fight
to feed on burst thistle.
Just three blooms,
the rest bract bulges
so plump they
bend to the ground.
Here, fritillaries frolic
and monarchs flitter.
Jupiter-spot Apollos
rest on larkspur,
as swallowtails soar.

All here for the fall's roar.
The tumult one minute after
a score, the crash below
of the devil's door.
Once Simba's squeak,
now the king's rumble.

It crashes fades of grey,
of melting mountains. Deeper,
the blue of shrunken glaciers.
It's Cervin and every peak,
the sole language they now speak.
It is froth and bubble, portents
of trouble—a course
that only roars true.

My World is a Kettle

It's one hundred degrees foreign
height. Shutters are shut, windows too.
But I'm living inside
a boiling kettle. Dripping
in the devil's dew. Champ
and stew. All day long I champ
and stew. I've missed you, after all
these years. I need your balm
for prickly, wickless red rash
boils and blisters.

I'm not allowed to use a knife
or anything sharp or pointed.
Everything slips from my grip.
I'm living outside reality,
the way rich folks do.

In this fever, each part of me grows
slowly. Except ear hair, sprouting
like the legs of a polar sea spider.
All I want is more time.

The Kitchen Holds

The wallpaper is white
and delft blue and does not peel.
The air is tiger red and fluorescent

brown. Cupboards, lemon
yellow as presses should be,
are dry with bread and biscuits.

Nobody opens them.
The day is as fast as a Donegal driver.
The towers in Siloam still fall.

The sky's too close to the sea.
A fly flees the bondage of a spider.
This Father dulls temptation,
but tests every day.

Le Chamossaire

The girl is black
and white from another
life. She reaches to add
a cobble to her cairn
eyes upward, narrow, fixed.

She's half a mile high
and fully biodegradable. She
is background to poses and pointing.
But backs turn on the main
display. The art

of God; Ta'aroa's backbone.
Spines, spires, scarps, of awe
and terror. A bumblebee yellow
biplane bisects the view. Glass

mountain lairs, homes
of superannuated rock
stars and still-alive racers
remind you: you're only passing

through. Here's not really for you.
Even the décor's born
in royal purple. The hitched skirts
of bluebells, birds-eye
primroses, toxic

foxglove. Our descent is dry
and dust and strained knees.
Gravity pulls and rut and decline
drag heads down. Down.
to the dry, dead dust.

Line in the Sahara Sand

The sky is apocalypse
goldenrod.
It is Sahara sand, carried
by the sweat of the sun
from Mali, Morocco
and Mauritania.

It lasts two days,
no more.
Border police order:
European dust only.
But it lives on
as falling blood rain
on chastened cars.

Dinosaurs Lived Longer Than You

Tiny arms and tiny brains.
You were vermin before the asteroid hit.
Dinosaurs lived longer than you.

Just an Anthropocene ape child,
craving repetition and novelty.
Dinosaurs lived longer than you.

Intelligent design, machine learning.
Editing earth and existence.
Dinosaurs lived longer than you.

A self-aware boiling frog
surfing on melted ice.
Dinosaurs lived longer than you.

Transhuman, terraforming:
Dinosaurs lived longer than you.

Orphaned Voyager, radio waves:
Dinosaurs lived longer than you.

Organ printing and AI:
Dinosaurs lived longer than you

Eternal plastic and chicken bones:
Dinosaurs lived longer than you.

Death by Black Tar

The meadows and moss and skin are straw
and sienna. Eons of green

blasted and bleached. We no longer count
the days, nothing is planted.

Brown oaks offer only ball bearings
as acorns. Rabbit-shaped trees

give piddling pears hanging
as earrings on coquettish branches.

A blue tit, crown slipping,
hovers but human feeders have no

nuts to offer. The earth
is dun, but, unlike us,

it will recover.

vii
little things

Lives Are Little Things

I've felt good things too I promise
myself. Moshing in dust in rare sun,
still a sweet child in Slane,
throwing myself to every song
I ever lived, against every friend
I ever loved. Or waiting
in the church with all who still sweep
the thickets and trouble from my path.
Waiting together for her—
pink, red, and ivory—
to walk my way.

And the days when nothing happened.
Never enough of those.
Speak of the angels
and they never appear.
The whole of two thousand and two
is a Robbie Keane goal and a white rabbit
pissing on stiff green IKEA bedclothes.
That's the last of it.
That's all of it.
Lives are little things.

Messi

Someone calls me from that place.
I will never say what. Or where.
That field, the green, the white.
The last thing I hear is them calling.
Your name over and over, *Messi, Messi...*

Softly, insistently they beckon.
You deliver: one swing of hip,
one shoulder drop, delicate dink.
Floodlights guide your journey.
The short way
         the only way
               your way.
Greatness glistens in gait-crushing gyrations.
Rosario, Catalonia. Nowhere. Never Seen.
Tell me where you are—and say no other name.

The King Is Red

Love never burns right.
I only see you in black
and white, tinged red.
Like Burns you turn
—on a sixpence—
folk songs into symphonies.

Cheeks ruddy as your shirt
you heave your hurdies against enemies.
Dance as others daze
untangle time
find space in black holes
weave tapestries with your toes.
Ever the seven from seventy-seven.

Seventy-eight. London's splendid baize
one sway,
weave, swerve,
merciless microchip.
Floodlights' pale beams
frame this perfect coup
that spark never parted joys.
Mersey banks break
eternal ecstasy erupts.
Long live the king,
the king is red
the king is red.

Cricket Ball

No new graces are blinked
into existence. The only sparks
in the stubble are our stumbles.

Life is a cricket ball in our grip.
Too large to be held in comfort
forcing and contorting us

with its hardness. The very
stitching the ever-there texture
beneath us. It is still so

pleasant to the softer touch,
inviting of our inconsequential
pressure. It is its heft that defines

it and us. The slippery solidity.
The weight of it, the weight between
us. It is much too heavy for what it is.

The Currach in the Caochan[3]

This hobble of being alive
bubble of strive and trouble.
Four score stream stretches
never too long. The past
composed, the future imperfect.

The currach on tangled caochan
pushing back through shrub
and scrub. Unmoored
by shivering shudders. Unmoved
by juddering quivers.

Float past pingle, moor, dingle.
Far from that bragging
cloud, from the splashing.
Cowed, you have two days left
being seven. Swim

on your back
without a kick.
Three days past forty-seven,
slip-stoning on the water's edge,
you find your voice

shanty sing the song they play
at your funeral. You need life
more than live it. You hum
the tune for all time.
The bobbles

---

[3] *Currach: a wooden-framed rowing boat traditionally used in the west of Ireland. Caochan: small stream (Scots)*

on the smooth run,
you hit them every time.
The laden lochs await
for your craft, for all
the flock flowing in.

About the Author

Adrian Harte a poet and writer from Monaghan, Ireland. His first book, a biography of rock band Faith No More entitled Small Victories (*Jawbone*), was published to critical acclaim in 2018.

His poetry has appeared in *Abridged, Peregrine Journal, Vita Poetica Journal, Beaver, Rabble Review,* and elsewhere. He lives in Aubonne, Switzerland.

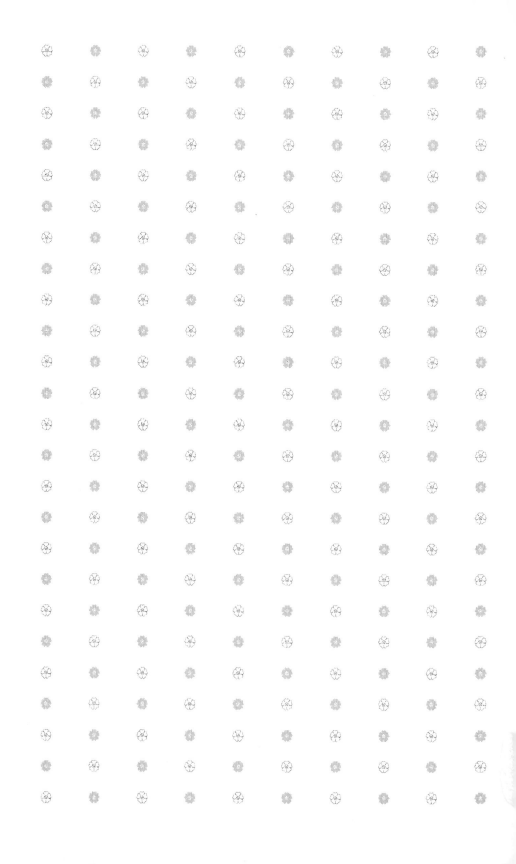

Printed in Great Britain
by Amazon

35706089R00079